This publication is designed to provide competent and reliable ideas regarding the subject matter covered. It is, however, sold with the understanding that the author and publisher is not engaged in rendering legal, financial or other professional advice. Laws typically vary from state to state and one should consult a legal or financial expert if assistance is required. The author and publisher disclaim any liability that is incurred from the use or application of the contents of the book.

Edited by Tina A. Swain for Imani Publishing

Copyright ©MMXII By Theodis Bland III.

All rights reserved.

Published by: Success Gene Publishing Inc.
Chicago, IL 60653

ISBN -13: 978-1479167302
ISBN – 10: 1479167304

First Edition

Cover designed: Arip Rahman

Dedicated to my Mother Barbara A. Bland, my Father Theodis Bland Jr. My grandfather, where I got my spirit of entrepreneurship, James NcNeil. My beautiful daughter DeAndria, this is for you. Special thanks to my lovely wife Tamela Bland, I couldn't have done this without you.

                                                    Theo

## Table of Contents

Chapter 1: Where is my cheese?..........................1

Chapter 2: Lessons from Haw................................8

Chapter 3: Lessons from Hem.............................21

Chapter 4: The Old Cheese Economy....................27

Chapter 5: The New Cheese Economy..................33

Chapter 6: Advantages of The New Cheese Economy.........................................................44

Chapter 7: The Role of Education in The New Cheese Economy......................................................49

Chapter 8: Why The 40/40/40 Plan is Financial Suicide...........................................................53

Chapter 9: The Politics of The Poor......................63

Chapter 10:  The Politics of The Rich.....................72

Chapter 11:  Industrial Revolutions..........................77

Chapter 12:  Summary of The Whole Matter.......80

Chapter 13:  Bonus Chapter: Getting Started.......83

## Prologue

"There is nothing permanent except change."

Fewer words have held their absoluteness than these words from Diogenes Laertius. Those who understand this truth are usually those who change with the times and advance throughout their lives. Those who resist the inevitable winds of change often become the victims of change. The New Cheese is the result of my own empirical perspective on change and how people respond to change. I was listening to one of the greatest success coaches of our day, Brian Tracy, in a workshop on the Laws of Self-Confidence and he told a story about an experiment that some researchers had conducted with Sammy the rat. Sammy was placed in a cage with four tunnels. The researchers had placed a piece of cheese at the mouth of the forth tunnel. Eventually, when Sammy was hungry, he looked for something to eat. Sammy found the cheese at the mouth of the fourth tunnel and was satisfied. Over a period of days the researchers conditioned Sammy to look for the cheese at the mouth of the fourth tunnel. Once he was conditioned to expect cheese at the mouth of the fourth tunnel the researchers changed the position of the cheese. It was still in the fourth tunnel but now the cheese was in the middle, not at the mouth. The change through Sammy off but he looked deeper into the tunnel and eventually found his cheese and was satisfied. The researchers then moved the cheese to the back of the tunnel and again Sammy worked his way to the back of the tunnel and got his cheese. Finally, the researchers moved the cheese out of the fourth tunnel altogether and placed it in the second tunnel. This change really confused Sammy. Yet he searched around the cage, he went between the tunnels, into the third tunnel and finally into the second tunnel where he found his cheese and was again satisfied. What the researchers concluded was that a rat, which has a brain the size of a pea or smaller knew that he, had to change with his conditions and eventually found his new cheese. Humans, who have the most complex brains in all of creation, will continue to go to and through tunnel four expecting to find cheese that is long gone and never coming back. After hearing this, I had what Oprah Winfrey calls an Ah ha moment! I knew that I had to remain vigilant and aware of the changes in society and it has served me well.

I want to offer just a word about the unlimited power of your human mind. Take a look around. Everything that you see came from the mind of another human being. Everything from

Prologue

Cars, Planes, Trains, Computers, Telephones, Cell Phones, Furniture, Appliances, etc all came from the human mind. Technology has advanced more in the last twenty five years than the last one thousand years. We are living in the age of ideas and with ideas come change. The good news is you own a human mind free and clear. It is standard equipment at birth and, in my opinion, the greatest gift from the creator. If you will commit to developing your mind nothing will be impossible to you. This century will produce more millionaires than all previous centuries combined. You only need to determine where you will stand in this new century of prosperity.  It will happen with or without you so I suggest you change with the times and take full advantage of the opportunities that this century will offer.  See you at the top!

Theo Bland

The future belongs to those who prepare for it.

Earl Nightingale

## Chapter 1: Where is my cheese?

In the early part of the new millennium, Dr. Spencer Johnson wrote a beautiful allegorical book called, "Who Moved My Cheese?" The book became a # 1 Best Seller. For anyone who hasn't had the opportunity of being exposed to the wisdom of Dr. Johnson, I will give you the Theo's Digest version of the story of "Who Moved My Cheese?" It is the story of four characters; two mice, Sniff and Scurry, and two little people, Hem and Haw. Essentially, the four characters live in a little maze town where they go out and get their cheese every day. The four characters represent traits found in all humans; the cheese represents whatever it is in life that we endeavor to achieve, be, do or have; and the maze represents life's circumstances and challenges.

The two mice, Sniff and Scurry, are just mice. They don't have any special skill, charisma or ability. They do, however, possess common sense factors that often evade humans. They tend to sniff out the cheese and take off running to find it. In the process, Sniff and Scurry run into dead-ends and brick walls, but that doesn't stop them.

Perhaps it's because the mice have never had anyone to tell them that those obstacles should stop them. Ultimately, Sniff and Scurry, with a sense of urgency, find a healthy supply of cheese in Cheese Station C. They also remained well prepared and aware in case anything changes in their circumstances.

On the other hand Hem and Haw are the opposite. Without a sense of urgency, they mosey out into the maze and stumble upon Cheese Station C. They even get comfortable with, what they see as, an endless supply of cheese. Hem and Haw

The New Cheese

settle in without a care in the world. Daily they lethargically head to Cheese Station C for their fill of cheese, never taking inventory of the fleeting supply.

One day the four characters arrive to find that Cheese Station C has been depleted, there is no more cheese. Immediately Sniff and Scurry take off to find more cheese. The two mice didn't waste time analyzing the situation; they simply knew that since the situation changed they needed to change as well. Hem and Haw were quite different. They spent the entire day murmuring and complaining about someone moving their cheese. Haw was a little more open to change than Hem. He had thoughts of going out to find new cheese, but Haw allowed Hem to convince him to wait and see if tomorrow new cheese would come. After a while with no new cheese, Haw decides to take off and go seek new cheese. Hem refuses to adjust and move on; he stays at Cheese Station C waiting for someone to bring more cheese.

In the meanwhile, Sniff and Scurry have found new cheese in Cheese Station N. Haw begins to experience little ah ha moments and sees the error of his old way of thinking. It takes a little time, but Haw finds little morsels of cheese and concludes that he is going in the right direction. He even returns to the village to tell Hem about what he has found. Even after receiving some cheese from Haw, Hem rejects the idea of setting out to find the new cheese. Haw again, takes his journey to find new cheese. Ultimately, Haw discovers a new cheese station with plenty of new cheese. Sniff, Scurry and Haw enjoy a life of new cheese and Haw has also become a better person in the process because he had to develop himself and adopt a new way of thinking.

    This story is so relevant to all of our lives today. Many of us know people like the characters in this story. We can quickly determine who's wise and who's foolish in this story and many of us would, perhaps, quickly conclude that we would be like Sniff and Scurry, who when the situation changes, so do we. And this may be true in some cases. I have found that many of us are not as pragmatic as we want to be in several areas of our lives. When it comes to the issues of career and money, however, many of us are like Hem and Haw and most of us are like Hem.

## Chapter 2: Lessons from Haw

There are many lessons to be learned from analyzing Haw. Haw represents the many people who realize that their circumstances have changed, but they don't know what to do initially. This happens to all of us at some point in life and if it hasn't happened to you yet, it will. What I like about Haw is the fact that he is open to new ideas. He may be a little delayed in taking action due to popular opinion and peer pressure, but eventually he cares more about finding new cheese than what people like Hem think. Anyone who will achieve anything of significance in life will have to overcome their self-limiting beliefs and fears. Over time, Haw got comfortable and never thought that his circumstances would change. News flash, in time, everything changes and the only way to last is to grow or evolve with changing conditions.

I must be clear. I'm speaking to the issue of change that is necessary for one to survive changing economic conditions, but the principle may certainly apply to other areas as well.

I would like to share my Haw experience with you! For many years I was a truck driver. When I started driving trucks, the money was really good. In fact, that was the reason why I started truck driving. I had my professional background in Radio Broadcasting, which was what I always wanted to do. But I found radio to be a revolving door and with a dynamic shift in the radio industry taking place, the cheese was being moved! I soon found myself unable to secure a job in the industry that I loved. My best friend at the time, Dee, often spoke of the money he was making on his job driving trucks. He suggested, along with another childhood friend Martez, that I get my CDL (Commercial Driver's License) and start a new career. I thought, "I have no better options, why not?" Immediately, I enrolled in the CDL Training Program at Olive Harvey College in Chicago and in just over two months, I was working for one of the largest carriers in the country and the best part was the job was local so I was home every night. I usually worked about seven or eight hours a night and very seldom went beyond that. The company paid me a salary of $200.00 per day and many days I only worked two hours. I was making more money than

I ever had in radio or anything else. I had arrived, so I thought.

After six months on the job, there were scuttlebutts of cuts and layoffs. I didn't have enough experience to go to another company that paid what I had become accustom to, so I did what most people did and waited till the very end and got my pink slip. Just like that, the rug was pulled from under me. I bounced around, looking for a job that would pay what I was used to getting, but I was never satisfied. I became what some people call a "Job Hopper." Let me address this. Some people tend to look at those who bounce around several jobs in a short period of time as unstable or unreliable. They think we can't commit. I must formally put you on notice that the reason many people get into this cycle, is because many times the "Job Hopper" hasn't resigned themselves to the idea of mediocrity and settling. We want more and won't quit until we get it. We may be a little misdirected as to what we should do, but we do know that we must do something. I want the critics to think about that the next time they think to themselves, "I hate my job, but I don't want to be a Job Hopper." The one thing that is stable about a

"Job Hopper" is they are not afraid to move with the cheese! So after a couple of years and about 6 jobs later (LOL) there was an opening at my former company AGAIN! I immediately called and got ready to return. I was back; everything was going to be the way it was before. Yeah right! Well, things were better than they had been for me while I was bouncing around, but the days of working seven or eight hours were a thing of the past. Instead of salary, now, they paid hourly. I could deal with that though. I would work twelve hours per day, sometimes more and I probably would have continued for many years, but the unthinkable happened. After six months back with the company, scuttlebutts returned. The hatchet man was coming around to make new cuts. I couldn't believe it. This time; I had experience, I wouldn't wait to get the pink slip, this time I gave them the pink slip, only mine was white, it was my resignation letter.

    I left the company on a Thursday and started working for another company Saturday. After four months with the new company, I was laid off. I couldn't seem to get a break. Someone kept moving my cheese.

Just like Haw, initially, I was full of self loathing and just hoping that someone would just simply put the damn cheese back. No one ever did. After a year, I started working for another trucking company and I noticed a pattern. Ever since that first cut, every job paid a little less and I had to do a little more. Now I was driving three hours round trip, in traffic, to get back and forth to work. With gas prices constantly increasing, I was spending more for gasoline than anything else. The company was taking advantage of me too. They controlled how much money I made and the amounts varied from day to day. I couldn't survive. This was when

I realized I was living on a modern day plantation and in fact, I was a modern day slave.

I'm told that Harriet Tubman, the revolutionary freedom fighter, once told a reporter that she "could have freed more slaves, if she could have only convinced them that they were slaves." There was a certain freedom that came with that realization that I was a modern day slave, because now I could do something about it. What made me a slave is the same thing that makes many Americans modern day slaves: If you work hard, just to give all of your earnings to someone else, in the form of bills, then you are a slave. The slave works hard all day every day, only to make someone else rich.  Yes, the slave master provides food, shelter and even clothing.  But so does your mortgage bank and credit card companies.  In order to do anything that I wanted to do, I had to get permission.  What does a slave have to do before doing anything he or she wants to do?  I think you get my point.  If someone else controls your cheese, then they also control you.

    I began to search for ways to extricate myself from the plantation.  It didn't happen overnight.  I stayed on the plantation while I searched for answers diligently.  Referring to my job became known as "The Plantation." Pretty soon, it became a standing joke between myself and my two brothers, Chris and Victor. Even my Dad began to call his job The Plantation.

Soon, it only made sense to study business trends and economics. I had to work to develop myself. I had to expand the circumference of my awareness. My favorite motivational speaker, Les Brown, says, "You don't get out of life what you want, you get out of life who you are. The good news is you can always become more by working to develop yourself." I was doing just that. I even tried to bring some of my friends and family along, but a lot like Harriet Tubman – I can't convince some people that they are slaves.

So the journey of Haw is sometimes a lonely one.  People don't understand why you start reading books about subjects that you've never cared about before.  They don't understand why you stop watching TV and listening to the radio but replace that activity with audio training CD's, tapes and DVD's.  Haw didn't really hang with Sniff and Scurry prior to the cheese crash, Hem was his running buddy.  But now that his mindset is different, Haw is running with people of like mind.  This is usually when your old friends say that you've changed.  And my reply is a resounding, "yes I have and you should too!"  But many never get it, so they get left behind just like Hem.

## Chapter 3: Lessons from Hem

It is quite unfortunate that many Americans fit the character of Hem but not many will readily admit the fact. Hem is the type who gets hyper comfortable in a situation to the point that the comfort level becomes entitlement. Hem was so accustomed to having cheese in the same place all the time that when times changed he refused to change with it. Hem did, however, have plenty of energy to complain about the situation. We see examples of this all the time. Everyone who is reading this book knows a Hem; in fact you may have been him at some point. I say "may have been", because after reading this book nobody has to remain in a Hem state. The sad thing is that even after reading this some of you will, until you internalize this message. There is a story that I love to share, I got it from Les Brown. He talks about walking past a porch where an old man sat with his dog. The dog was moaning and groaning and a young man asked, "What's wrong with the dog?" The old man said, "He's lying on a nail." "Why won't he get up?" The young man asked. The old man answered, "Because it doesn't hurt badly enough." The reality is people like Hem have enough energy and dissatisfaction to keep complaining but they are not moved to take action.

Anyone who doesn't have the vision or desire to make their lives better is a sad case. Yet there is still a level of what I call "Loser-ism" that goes a step lower. Not only did Hem not want to go find new cheese for himself, but he tries to hold Haw back from going as well. So if you are not Hem, then you need to identify who is Hem in your life and run in the opposite direction. If you hang with Losers the best you can ever hope to be is the best Loser, but still a Loser. Haw decided to break away from his Loser friend and eventually not only found new cheese but he also found new friends in Sniff and Scurry. I don't use the term Loser in a disrespectful manner, I'm simply talking about the cycle of inactivity that leads to not accomplishing anything significant for oneself.

A notable reason why Hem didn't want to venture out into the maze and find new cheese was because of fear. Hem fed his fear by constantly focusing on what negative things could happen. Things like, what if we don't find any new cheese out there. Somehow, we have been led to believe that playing it safe leads to something worthwhile. This reminds me of a story I once heard, it goes something like this. There was a soldier captured during a war and he was due to be executed by a firing squad. But the opposition decided to give him a chance to leave. He was brought into a room with a door and given the opportunity to leave. The soldier asked what's on the other side of the door and the commander told him a world of untold horrors. The soldier opted to die by the firing squad. After the execution another soldier asked what's really on the other side of that door and the commander answered Freedom. Some people would actually rather face a firing squad then take their chances in a world of the unknown.

Hem was destined to starve to death if he stayed in Cheese Station C but somehow that wasn't enough motivation to move him to action. I see people all the time, who hate their jobs, hate their bosses and hate their co-workers, but faithfully show up to work. People are committed, not only to what they don't like doing but also what does not provide an adequate living for them or their families, yet they won't bother to look at other options.

## Chapter 4: Old Cheese Economy

During the 235 year history of the United States, the country has experienced many shifts in the economy.  At one point the U.S. economy was driven by agriculture.  We moved through agriculture into a strong industrial economy and then into a service and information based economy.  With every shift there was job loss and elimination.  Technological advances are great for capitalists but not so great for employees.   This is where one would be prudent to see the handwriting on the wall or smell the cheese often so you can tell when it's old.

Right now there are pseudo-intellectuals and armchair economists sitting around talking about when the economy recovers. I hear it all the time; in academic settings, barber shops, and religious settings. People are really waiting for the government to pass a certain law or create something to force businesses to give them jobs. I need to help my fellow Americans understand that when the economy shifts there is no bringing jobs back. Think about it! There once was a position called elevator operator. When Otis and other manufacturers created self serve elevators people lost jobs and those jobs never came back. Technology is great, but the downside for someone with an employee mindset is they don't have control of their cheese.

The days of the 40/40/40 plan are over. For those who don't know what the 40/40/40 plan is, that's when you work 40 hours per week for 40 years and retire on 40% of what you use to make. We no longer live in a world where we compete with our neighbors and classmates for jobs. We truly live in a global community and you are competing with global neighbors for work. This new economic system calls for you to develop new skills applicable to competitive industries. You need more than one skill and more than one language. Essentially, you must become more valuable.

We have had good cheese in our jobs for a long time, but the cheese has moved. The opportunities of the twenty first century are not in being an employee, the opportunities are in business. You may be thinking, but I don't have a business, now you know why you don't have any cheese. We will fully discuss business ownership and why now is the best time to start a business in the next chapter. Robert Kiyosaki, author of Rich

Dad Poor Dad, talks about changing your value system in order to get rich and right now that's what Americans will have to do in this new century. Most Americans are taught, growing up; to go to school, get good grades so that you can get a good JOB. But what else can they teach their child if that's all they've ever known. A slave can't teach anyone about freedom when all they've ever known is bondage. Therefore, you can't get sound advice about business or opportunities from people who've never had them or taken advantage of them.

Rest assured of one thing, the idea of a safe and secure job is an old idea of the past and it will not return. So my advice is to start looking for new cheese. If you happen to be someone who still has a decent paying job or any job at all, then you need to start searching for new cheese before your supply dries up. New cheese doesn't mean go look for another job, new cheese means deconstructing the entire idea of a job and constructing a new paradigm – a paradigm of ownership.

## Chapter 5: The New Cheese Economy

In the last chapter, I talked about business ownership being the new cheese. This entire chapter will be dedicated to showing you why the new economy will demand that you become a business owner. The age of the Independent Entrepreneur via the home based business is what we are moving into. The average person does not have the working capital and probably can't qualify for a business loan from a bank in order to start a traditional business. Plus, starting a traditional business is far more risky for anyone who has no prior experience in running a successful operation. There are, however, more opportunities than ever before in the area of Direct Sales, MLM or Network Marketing. Network Marketing has produced more self made millionaires than any other industry, including real estate.

One way of determining what you should do in a given a situation is by watching what other successful people are doing. Some of the biggest names in business are either involved with Network Marketing or highly recommend it. Both Donald Trump and Warren Buffet own MLM companies. Robert Kiyosaki recommends everyone get involved in MLM. I even have a MLM business and as I look around, I see more and more prominent figures getting involved. Former Chicago Mayoral Candidate William "Dock" Walls is involved with the industry. Chicago TV personality Garrard McClendon is in the MLM industry. NBA legend Dominique Wilkins is in the MLM industry. These are people who have experienced huge success in their careers and if they can see the value in launching their own MLM business; how is it that someone working a regular nine to five barely making ends meet can't?

You see, the New Cheese economy requires that you lose pride and realize that no matter how educated you are, no matter how many degrees you have and no matter how much you know about your job – companies don't reward you for that in the New Cheese economy. What matters in the New Cheese economy is LEADERSHIP! In the Old Cheese economy, you were paid not to think. As long as you showed up to work and did what you were told to do, you were rewarded. Companies don't want to have to pay employees a guaranteed amount of money for an unguaranteed amount of production. From a business perspective, this only makes sense. Why should I pay you twenty dollars per hour and your goal is to do as little work as possible. Now, I'm not saying that this is the attitude of every employee. I know some employees who work extremely hard for their companies. I also know far more employees who go to work and find every way possible to skate out of responsibility. I'm just talking about the amount of money companies spend on wages. If we add the cost of benefits and retirement plans, it gets far more expensive. I think companies are partly to blame, however, because they failed to train leaders. Instead they wanted obedient workers/followers. Many of us have been in situations where we were instructed to do things that made no sense and perhaps cost the company more as opposed to allowing the experts, you who do the work daily, to come up with more feasible solutions that would be more efficient and cost effective. But in a robotic culture, thinking is not allowed and not promoting leadership is also a form of bad leadership. At any rate, this is where we are now. This situation has changed. The good news is that there is plenty of opportunity for someone who always knew that they had more talent to offer than their job allowed them to develop and utilize. Now you have the opportunity to cut the leash and develop your skills and abilities and get paid what you think you are worth as opposed to what someone else thinks you are worth.

Many of you have always known that you could make better decisions than your boss or manager or supervisor. Because of all the "isms" of the Old Cheese economy you may have experienced unfair disadvantages like: racism, sexism, classism, nepotism, or ageism; none of which have a stronghold in the New Cheese economy. For the first time in life, many Americans are on a level playing field.

## Chapter 6: Advantages of the New Cheese Economy

Under the old system, there was discrimination everywhere. Consider, if you will, a person who may have made a bad decision as a teenager. This person may have gotten involved with the wrong crowd, been at the wrong place at the wrong time, or could have been a flat out criminal. Either way under the Old Cheese economy, due to convictions that may have been legitimate or not, ex convicts didn't have a chance to get back on their feet. This led to high rates of recidivism and perhaps robbed some companies' of great employees who would have worked very hard.

Well, in the New Cheese economy, this doesn't have to be the case. Everyone can have a new start. There are no excuses in the new economy, you either want more out of life or you don't. Many people working a job will never have friends who are millionaires. Again, I must stress, you can never truly learn how to get more out of life if you're only around people who never had more. Studies have shown that your income is the average of your top 5 friends. It's safe to say that if you want more out of life you need to find people who are where you want to be and learn from them, Yes or Yes?

Another advantage of the New Cheese economy is you don't have to have a boss. There are many more opportunities to be your own boss. As an entrepreneur, you determine how you will do things; keep in mind, you only eat what you kill. For the true leader this is a great thing, but for someone who doesn't want to write their own ticket, that's a nightmare. The reality of the New Cheese economy, however, is that if one chooses to stay in the mindset of the Old Cheese economy they will suffer great loss. The jobs that remain in

## Advantages of the New Cheese Economy

America will be consolidated, many being part-time with no benefits. Many employees already feel over worked and under paid. Well those who refuse to evolve with the New Cheese economy will really feel over worked and under paid.

The greatest aspect of the New Cheese economy is a revolutionary compensation plan. All employees are use to what is known as linear income. Essentially, linear income works like this: a worker exchanges hours for dollars. Only one person is responsible for generating your income, YOU. If and when you stop working you stop earning. That is linear income. I can tell you now that your boss doesn't get rich because he believes in linear income.  What your boss believes in is known as leverage.  Leverage is a wealth structure.  A leverage situation is when you have a team of people that generate income and you get a small piece of what they produce.  Think about it this way; you and forty nine other employee's work for Mr. Boss, all fifty of you generate twenty five dollars in revenue per hour, but Mr. Boss gets five dollars per hour from each of you.  You still get twenty dollars an hour, but you are linear.  Let's do the math. In a regular forty hour work week you make $800 dollars for the week, $20/hr x 40 hours

= $800. This is linear income. Mr. Boss who only gets five dollars per hour on each employee gets $10,000 for the week, $5/hr x 2000 hours = $10,000. This is leverage income. You decide which is better; I know the one I want!

| Employee | 40HRS | x | $20/HR | $800 |
| --- | --- | --- | --- | --- |
| Boss | 2000HRS | x | $5/HR | $10,000 |

This is the power of the New Cheese economy. I'm here to tell you that not only is this New Cheese, but it's better cheese. You don't have to be an expert in the New Cheese economy, because the experts are going to teach you everything you need to know to get where they are. Under the Old Cheese, people had to suppress information to get ahead or stay ahead. But under the New Cheese, it's to a person's advantage to share every secret to success because, the better you do the better I do – even if you pass me, I benefit! Talk about a win/win situation. This system has been around for a long time, but many of you were too comfortable to even take a look at it. Some of you took a look and may have even gotten involved, but didn't take it serious and quit. You even convinced yourself that it didn't work; it's a pyramid scam and a bunch of other excuses. The truth is you didn't work. Many of us took a look, got involved and people said we were stupid or that it doesn't work, etc. Now they see our lifestyle and say, "THAT WORKS?" I love to say, "It works, you work, I DON'T."

In the New Cheese economy, people are going to beg you to show them an opportunity. In fact, the new normal will be operating a home based business of some sort. The oddballs will be the people who still work a job.

## Chapter 7: The Role of Education in the New Cheese Economy

Many of you are wondering, what about attending college or what about my degrees? Under the Old Cheese economy, you were rewarded for simply going to school for at least four years, obtaining a degree and even going back for more. I know too many people with degrees and no concrete understanding of their field. I had friends who had degrees and would readily admit that they knew nothing about the subject. I'm sure that they were exaggerating a little, but there was definitely an element of truth to the statement. They were able to get "good jobs," however, just because they had the degree. Well, that day is over too. Does this mean one shouldn't attend college? Of course not! But that does mean one has to change the objective of college.

Information is the currency of the New Cheese economy. This means that education must be used to enhance one's value to the marketplace. Zig Ziglar says, "You can have everything you want if you'll help enough other people get what they want." Your education has to be focused on what does the market want. The market simply means the population. What is it that the world wants or need? You find a way to deliver it and you will be compensated. I decided to use my education to become an authority on business and economics. This is a subject that many people often run from but everyone is involved with. If you need to know how to start or build a business, I am the expert. I teach other people how to do this and the marketplace rewards me for it. This goes back to what I talked about in chapter four relative to developing new skills.

Degrees can be used to offer up front credibility, but ultimately one will have to demonstrate the necessary know how to build trust with the marketplace. People will pay you to teach them what you know when they know the knowledge will help them get to their destination. So continuing education is a great thing as long as the objective is to become the expert and authority on the subject and not to get a job.

## Chapter 8: Why the 40/40/40 Plan is Financial Suicide

Earlier we talked about the 40/40/40 plan, now I want to further explain why a job is absolutely financial suicide. Let's analyze the plan, so you can see exactly why it cannot work forever.

Let's say that Employee A starts working at the age of twenty-three for Company ABC. Also, Employee A has just graduated from University XYZ and they have $40,000.00 dollars of student loan debt. Although Employee A has a degree, they are still an entry level worker so their starting salary is

$33,000.00 per year. Employee A is planning to work hard and rise through the ranks and build a solid career with Company ABC, therefore they invest in the company's 401K and full benefits package. With the added benefits, plus the tax burden, Employee A's take home pay is around $25,000 per year. Now let's build from there.

Employee A rents a studio for about $600.00 per month with all utilities included. Let's say that all of the monthly expenses total $1,000.00. Based on these numbers Employee A will have about $1,100 remaining. Of the remaining funds, they save half and invest half. Employee A will save over $13,000.00 dollars in two years. Employee A then decides to marry their college romance. Now Employee A needs the savings for a down payment on a home that costs $250,000.00. Employee A's spouse makes the same amount of money and has the same disciplines with their money, but they have depleted their savings paying for a wedding with all the trimmings and their new house. By the way, the mortgage on the new home in about $2,000 per month, this includes insurance. Now the couple needs the $600.00 from the former studio rent and they can't afford to save at the moment because they need to use the $550.00, towards the mortgage as well. The spouse, who makes the same amount with the same disciplines, will have to contribute the same amount to the house in order to cover the mortgage and possibly utilities. One of them will need to scale back on their investments because they will have other expenses like food and transportation. So as you can see, just trying to get a piece of the American dream for Employee A is starting to push them into a negative net worth. Once children come into the picture this couple will be in debt and the financial treadmill will be in full effect.

This is usually the part where Employee's start demanding raises. The truth of the matter is even if they both get raises; the raises won't be significant enough to keep up with their expenses. Then the occasional furnace or hot water tank problem, car breakdown and any other inconvenience only makes the situation worse. Let's say that the couple manages to get raises over the next few years and now instead of $33,000.00, now they make $40,000.00 a piece. They have gained an additional $14,000.00 dollars per year, but now they are in another tax bracket so they actually only gained about $10-11,000.00 and this may be just enough to allow the couple to tread until some major event happens and trust me, a major event always happens. And the truth of the matter is, that raise that we look forward to is often not an increase when you consider inflation.

We are only talking about living day to day and these are relatively ideal conditions. We know that things are usually less than ideal. Now let's fast forward to retirement. This couple barely got by while they worked, but now they must live on less. Let's say that the couple managed to get their salaries up to $100,000.00 total, in retirement it will drop to about $40,000.00. Remember now, they also had some investments. Figure over the years with market volatility and inflation, those investments yield an additional $1,000.00 per month, so now they have about $52,000.00 annual income for retirement. Provided they never refinanced their home, which is not likely, the house may be paid off. As long as they don't experience any major health challenges, they may be slightly secure for retirement. The only problem is most couples fortunes don't work this way.

Most companies don't have positions that allow employees to enter and remain for forty years with decent raises over the years. Most couples won't have equal salaries or better. Most couples will get deeper into debt every year because they want to take lavish vacations, buy timeshares and expensive cars. As for retirement plans and pensions; one of the problems with pensions is it creates a liability for the company while paying current employees for their labor. This is a dynamic that cannot be sustained for a long period of time. As more and more people retire, the company has more pensions to pay. They will eventually find themselves paying more to former employees than current employees so current employees suffer because the company can't offer high wages.  The company will then begin over charging its customers to make up the money it's losing on pensions.  Soon the company is insolvent and bankrupt.  Now nobody is getting anything.  This is why many companies switched from Defined Benefits retirement packages to Defined Contributions retirement packages.  So most employees will have to work just to fund their retirement accounts, which mean they struggle during their working years.

    I'm not saying that working is bad; I'm saying that if your only plan is to work for Company ABC, then you are setting yourself up to fail financially. If one is committed to the 40/40/40 plan, then one must have a Plan B.

## Chapter 9: The Politics of the Poor

Every four years, when the United States goes to the polls and elects a President, the battle wages between the haves and the have not's. On one side, a candidate makes promises that he claims will explicitly help a particular segment of the population and by default help other segments of the population. Another candidate campaigns on promises to help another segment of the population and subsequently, by default, other segments will also gain. This has been the ebb and flow of politics since the beginning of political parties and it won't change any time soon. What has to change is the way you interact with it.

The reason why Washington DC is rampant with lobbyists and it seems as though politicians are mostly bought and paid for is because some people have used their influence and financial power to push for laws and rules that help their cause. The rich and powerful know how to come together and practice what is called, in Swahili, Ujima or collective work and responsibility. It's typically the poor who do not practice this principle. The first message that the poor and working class need to understand is that there is nothing holding them back. There is no politician that you can elect to make your dreams come true or give you the American Dream. There is no political savior who will rise to power and make your problems dissipate. Notice that many politicians have come and gone, community and political activists that have been around for 40 years or more are still singing the same tune that they sung in the turbulent 1960's and the masses of poor and working class still have little or nothing to show for the struggle. Maybe this is a sign that we as a people will not make it to the Promised Land, but I can tell you that YOU as an individual can!

The poor must change their politics. Since politics is essentially the process that determines who gets what, when, and how. All the poor has to do is look at who is getting what, when, and how they get it; and position themselves to get their share. This is not an over simplification of a complexity beyond your ability. In fact all you need is a few changes in your value system; learn a new skill or two and the motivation to get more out of life. You see, the true purpose of Government is to protect your rights, not to give you rights. For too long the poor have said things like, "they are cutting welfare" or "they are cutting unemployment." First consider who are "they" and what are "they" really doing. They are the political leaders that this country has elected to govern. They are also, in many cases, limiting the overextended powers that they have given to themselves in order to help the less fortunate. Remember, it was never the Government's role, to feed those who didn't go out and find food for themselves or house those who didn't get out and build their own shelter. I do admit that the Government should have bore some responsibility to the descendants of African Slaves and those in the first two or three generations of reconstruction.

I say that because, it was the failure of the Government to protect the rights of Blacks in America from 1865 – 1965. There were, however, some who in spite of the challenges of those times that accomplished great things. In short, it is not the responsibility of the Government to give you anything; it is the Government's responsibility to protect your rights. So how does this apply to the new cheese? I'm glad you asked!

Think about your rights. There are three rights that Thomas Jefferson explicitly named in a sacred document we call The Declaration of Independence: The right to Life, Liberty and the

Pursuit of Happiness. The Government must protect those rights. You don't have the right to Food or Food Stamps, Housing or Section 8, Employment or Raises. But your rights are worth so much more than what you've been fighting for. It's the difference between fighting for a piece of fish and fighting for the ocean that contains an assortment of sea life. Poor people have been fighting for a piece of fish for centuries and still complain when they get it. Because, after they get the piece of fish, they consume it and have to fight for more. But if they pursued their own fishing pole and pond, they would never have to fight for a piece of fish again. My challenge to the poor is to stop chasing that which is cheap and temporal. It's time to think on a higher level.

If there are twenty to thirty people working in a factory, that group of people can begin working together to pool some of their resources and skills together and start their own business in the same industry. The workers are the experts because they are the ones doing the job. Even if the jobs are compartmentalized, when everyone comes to the table, all the necessary skills will be present. Of course there are things that must be researched and covered in order to make this happen, but the idea should be enough to light a fire under people who want more out of life.  This idea can work in any industry.  The main idea is simply, poor people must shift their thinking from "do for me" to "do for self."

## Chapter: 10 The Politics of the Rich

The politics of the rich is quite different from the poor. I stated in the previous chapter that the rich and powerful know how to practice Ujima. Simply put, they realize that their money and resources provide the leverage they need to make the political system work for them. They don't care who is elected because they have the means to lobby and work the system. I don't see this as good or bad, I just see this as the reality of how things work. The rich and powerful have organizations, PACS (Political Action Committees) and special

Interests and other groups that focus on the agenda of the rich. Although the poor have the same things, the goals of the organizations working for the poor are a little different.

The goals for the rich are to have the government allow them to keep more of their money through low taxes and as little government involvement as possible in their affairs. There are others, but these are the main goals. The rich push for laws that make it easier for them to effect industry. One of the hottest issues of 2011 was the Wisconsin battle between Governor Scott Walker and the Public Workers and their ability to collectively bargain. It is believed that the Governor's decision to go after the Public Employees was effected by the Koch Brothers. This is just an example of how the system works. The rich back their candidate and when the candidate wins the election he or she will do the bidding of those who got him or her elected. This goes on all over the country and even at the national level.

Politicians come and go, but industry is here to stay. When I was in the Marine Corps, there were times when a new OIC (Officer In Charge) would come in to my unit. During these times, you could see the old school Master Sergeant, diplomatically, try to manipulate the new OIC. The thinking was along the lines of, I have ran this unit the way I wanted for years and I will continue to be here, you may only be here for one year, if that, so I won't let you come in and change what I have established. This only works with a young $2^{nd}$ or $1^{st}$ Lieutenant. After an officer has been around for a while, he or she is hip to the game. Similarly, politicians work the same way. Old politicians sometimes get new politicians to sell out their constituency to special interest in exchange for a long lucrative career. This happens in both major political parties. My advice is to get involved and more importantly, get on the side that you can benefit from. You can never go wrong with a "do for self" attitude. On the other hand, if you are dependent on the government for your living, you are in bad shape. The new cheese is always a result of innovation and technological advances. This allows businesses to increase their bottom line by increased production at a lower cost. Simply put, its good business. The rich are only doing for themselves what is beneficial for them and their family and friends. Now you have to begin to think in a similar way and do what is best for you and your family and friends.

## Chapter: 11 Industrial Revolutions

Throughout the course of history, technology has always moved society forward.  And society as a whole is usually better because of it.  I'm not a historian, but I do know a little something about history.  In the early part of the nineteenth century in Europe, Great Britain experienced an industrial revolution.  Before the steam engine and the advent of factories and mass production, individuals could make their living from just about anything: Farming, Gunsmith, Candle maker, Tailor/Seamstress, etc.  As factories began to spring up, many people were forced to work in them because they could not compete with mass production. Mass production also allowed businesses to sell products for a cheaper price than what an individual could charge. There was resentment of the factory even to the extent that some would go out at night and break into the factories and vandalize the machines. Ultimately, they were jailed and the innovations continued.

Time always brings about change. In fact, change is perhaps the one thing that is a sure constant in life, outside of death. The world is experiencing another revolution. I say the world because economies are so interrelated and connected now that what happens in one country could affect others in another country for good or bad. The jobs that are being eliminated now will never return, so a wise person will do well to look ahead at what may emerge in the new economy and beat everyone else to it or start creating your own empire.

## Chapter: 12 Summary of the Matter

Quite simply, Dr. Johnson gave a wakeup call for us to take note of our own behavior. I'm here to let you know that the cheese is gone, but you still have time to go find new cheese if you act now. The new cheese will not look like the old cheese because the old cheese is, well, old. Businesses don't want to pay people high guaranteed wages for unpredictable levels of productivity and sales. This means that you must create your own opportunities and trust me; there are many available to you.

These changes are not "if" but "when." They are not "optional" but "mandatory." The days of getting a job and working the same job for thirty or forty years is a thing of the past. There will be no defined retirement plans, in the new cheese economy; you will eat what you kill, so you must become a great hunter. The jobs of the twenty first century are low paying and insecure, so if that is something that you are fine with, then I am fine with you being fine with it. But for the people who want more than 10-15 dollars an hour you will have to work to develop yourself so that you can become more valuable to the marketplace. I will tell you exactly what you need to do in the final chapter. Keep in mind that the costs of living will continue to increase, so if your wages don't keep up with rising costs you will be in financial ruin. This information is only to sound the alarm for the average person that is not aware of this and may believe that there will be an economic recovery and everything will go back to normal, there will be a new normal and you most likely won't like it.

Chapter: 13 What You Can and Should Do Now

If you have taken to heart the things written in this book, you are already going in the right direction. The next thing you must do is change the way you think about money and how you get it. You can no longer think like an employee, from now on you are an entrepreneur. You create your own opportunities.

You need to adopt a personal empowerment regiment. Simply put, you are embarking on a new lifestyle and you will need encouragement, direction and new education to stay the course and succeed. Every morning you should start your day with positive and inspiring messages. I suggest you get my audio CD's that help to coach you through the start of your new lifestyle. Other benefits would be to: attend workshops, seminars, and training events that will expose you to new leaders in business and self development. You will notice that there is another type of education that you will receive and find it essential to your success.

 Set worthy goals. Earl Nightingale says, "Success is the progressive realization of a worthy ideal." Begin to think about what you really want to do, be, and have in life.  Know that there are no limits on your life, so you must take the limits - that you have imposed on yourself - off.  If you want to be an author, filmmaker, playwright, own a business, etc you can do it.  I want you to write down everything you want to do occupationally speaking.  After you have the list of things, find the one thing that you want to do or accomplish more than anything else on that list and circle it.  This is going to be the area you focus all your energy on until you complete it.  Then you can start the process all over again to find your next area of focus.  After you find what you want to focus on set a date by which you want to achieve that thing and write it down on another sheet of paper.

Here is an example: "By June 16, 2011, I am a published author." Now that you have written your goal and put a date on it, write down what you will need to make it happen. This will become your execution plan. Write down who you will need to help you accomplish this goal. You should also write down the foreseen challenges and obstacles that you think may arise, this way you can deal with them before they show up. Now your worthy goal is written and you have a plan in place to accomplish it. Believe that you will accomplish your goal and believe that you deserve to have what you have written; because you will and you do.

Now follow your daily empowerment regiment. Listen to positive, inspirational and informational CD's in the morning while getting ready to start your day, do the same in the car. No more WGCI, V103 or WGN radio or whatever the popular stations are in your city. The fact is this; Steve Harvey, Tom Joyner, Ryan Seacrest, Howard Stern, Rush Limbaugh and others are already living their dreams, now you must get in position to live yours. You can go back to listening to them when you are rich like them! No negativity for the time being, that means no news. I know that may seem odd, but trust me, when something happens that you need to know someone will call you or you will hear about it in the grocery store or what have you. You have to think on a higher frequency and bad news along with foolish conversation only diminishes inspired thought. Read your goal when you wake in the morning, read it throughout the day and make it the last thing you read before going to sleep at night. You become what you think about most, so you want this goal to dominate your thoughts.

You may need to eliminate negative friends and family members or don't share your goals with them, because you are different now. People will laugh at you and say disheartening things to you. They don't really mean any harm, but it's all they know to do. Deep down inside, they are praying you will succeed because this will give them hope for their lives or they think they can borrow money from you when you come into yours!

I would also join a network marketing company to develop business skills and posture. These companies are great for developing leadership skills; quite frankly I see these

6. Zig Ziglar

Here are some books that I recommend you read as well:

1. The Secret: Rhonda Byrne

2. Think and Grow Rich: Napoleon Hill

3. The Power of the Subconscious Mind: Joseph Murphy

These teachings will lead you to more. I am excited about your new lifestyle and I am looking forward to seeing you enjoying the new cheese perhaps on the beaches of the world. Remember, you deserve to live your best life, now go out there and make it happen!

opportunities as self development programs with compensation plans. You will attract a new circle of friends who are like minded and supportive, not to mention you can actually make some serious money.

Here is a list of people that I would Google to listen to what they have to say about your new lifestyle:

1. Les Brown
2. Earl Nightingale
3. Brian Tracy
4. W.C. Stone
5. Joseph Murphy

## Other Books from the Author:

*The Success Guide for the Unstoppable Entrepreneur.*

## Audio Products from the Author:

*The Magic of Mentoring: Are you getting the most from your Mentor?*

*Flight Plan: Success is by Choice, Not Chance.*

www.TheoBlandOnline.info

www.ingramcontent.com/pod-product-compliance
Lightning Source LLC
Chambersburg PA
CBHW061513180526
45171CB00001B/168